Praise for *A Rope of Luna* by Lisha Adela García

"Bold, fresh, painful, and charged with spiritual energy, Garcia's A Rope of Luna pulls us through the cycles of life with insight, passion, and "the stubbornness of a heel ground into the dirt." Poignant and sweet in its intimacy, this collection of poems immerses us in the raw wound of life as an immigrant child, as a daughter of a dying mother, as an estranged child of a faraway father, of a determined poet capturing the beauty of life in its "new botanical garden where I choose the order of petal and plant." Vividly painting the experience of leaving her native land and of being immersed in a place where her ethnicity, her language, and the prejudice of local institutions mark her as the despised and the disposable, Garcia evokes an eloquence both powerful and incisive, describing her laws of survival as "You bury screams in the dirt, and can't move....An unseen raptor....bites off the appendages of all you once knew to be true." A must-read volume!"

— Dr. Carmen Tafolla, State Poet Laureate, Texas

"As a rope is woven of strands and made stronger by such weaving, the strengths of this meticulously crafted book of poems accrete and then remain with the reader. In her poem "Shard," Lisha Garcia writes, "Daughter-Love-Sister-Mother/ is a broken shard next to an ancient ruin./ A geometric pattern/ displaced from the whole." The poet's knowledge of familial patterns and shattering exile haunts these vivid, lucid poems."

— Dr. Natasha Sajé, Curator of the Anne Newman Sutton Poetry series, Utah Book Award winner and Director of Creative Writing Program at Westminster College in Salt Lake City. Author of: *Vivarium*, Tupelo Press

"Lisha Adela Garcia's poems are passionate and primal. Her vision transcends the personal, and she speaks in the voice of her community – Mexican-American immigrants whose voices are marginalized and need to be heard. These are blow the roof off, burn the house down poems. At this time in our history, *A Rope of Luna* is a voice that must be heard!"

— Diane Frank, Author of *Canon for Bears and Ponderosa Pines*

"There are many kinds of exile — the exile of immigration forced, as with this poet, without warning from one's home country, as well as exile within families due to cruelty, estrangement, and loss. But by turning to nature and the moon, Garcia finds solace — from racist bullying in "the refuge of trees" or, by journey's end, in a "haloed moon" whose aura is "a sanctuary...a haven of even breaths." In lustrous, nature-drenched language, Garcia unflinchingly examines the stages of a woman's life, sets "grief ablaze," charts the way the "life force battles/to stay upright," and dives deep, as if into Mayan *cenotes*, to claim the *duende* that is her due."

— Dr. Terry Blackhawk, Founder, InsideOut Literary Arts
Project; Kresge Arts in Detroit Literary Fellow

A ROPE OF LUNA

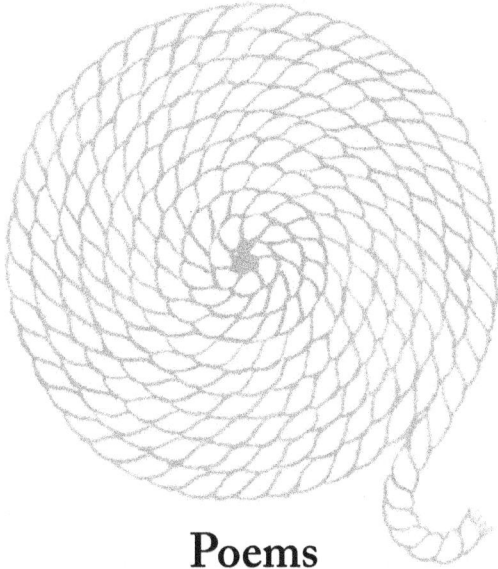

Poems
by
Lisha Adela García

BLUE LIGHT PRESS ◆ 1ST WORLD PUBLISHING

SAN FRANCISCO ◆ FAIRFIELD ◆ DELHI

A ROPE OF LUNA

Copyright ©2018 by Lisha Adela García

1st World Library
PO Box 2211
Fairfield, IA 52556
www.1stworldpublishing.com

Blue Light Press
www.bluelightpress.com
bluelightpress@aol.com

Book & Cover Design
Melanie Gendron
melaniegendron999@gmail.com

Cover Art
"In Memory of Patricia" © 2018, Melanie Gendron

Author Photo
Melissa Evans, Melissa Raelynn Photography

First Edition

Library of Congress Control Number: 2018936014

ISBN 9781421838045

For the family dead on my *Altar de Muertos*:
Mother, Father, *Abuelos*, Brother, *Tíos* and *Tías*

In memory of Susana Romero de González,
mi Tía y segunda madre, and my much loved
Tío Juancho who misses her and is equally loved.

In memoriam, and with much love to the poet soul of
Emilio Hinojosa, my beloved *Tío*.

For all of my ancestors, guardian spirits,
angels, *duendes* and ghosts.

Mil Gracias to Terry Blackhawk, Natasha Sajé,
and Carmen Tafolla, for their encouragement over
the years and writing an endorsement for the book.

In Gratitude:

In gratitude to Diane Frank and all of the Blue Light Press writing groups who have seen the dance on these pages in various iterations. In gratitude to Patricia Smith, Jo Reyes Boitel and Sheila Black who with much dedication and respect read and edited the manuscript during different phases of its life. With much appreciation to the support of Suzanne Dudley Schon, mi hermanita Dominicana, for her unwavering support of my journey. Thanks to Jennifer Clement and the San Miguel writers for keeping me going and rewinding so many of these poems. Mil Gracias to Terry Blackhawk, Natasha Sajé, and Carmen Tafolla, for their encouragement over the years and writing a blurb for the book.

"The one experience that all humans share is grief,
and it takes the right kind of poetry to set grief ablaze."

— Malidoma Patrice Somé

"When fortune dictated that I also be a poet,
I imposed upon myself the secret obligation
of defining the moon."

— Jorge Luis Borges

TABLE OF CONTENTS

SECTION 1: SPLIT IN TWO

SECTION 2: THE GOOD DAUGHTER

SECTION 3: IF NOT, WINTER

SECTION 4: GATHER

End

SECTION 1

SPLIT IN TWO

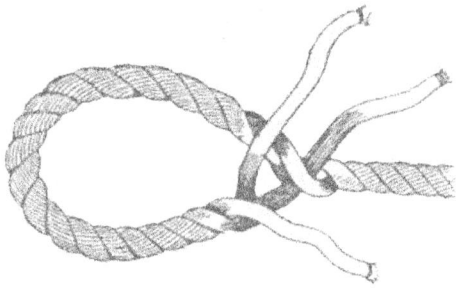

Age 6, First Mother Shattering

Mamá said:

> *You don't need to hold my hand*
> *I am busy.*
>
> *We won't be coming back,*
> *say goodbye.*
>
> *Quit staring at the moon, choose three toys*
> *we are leaving México.*
>
> *Where are we going, how can I pick?*

The Day We Split in Two — Entering the USA

You'll learn English and the proper way to say, "Yes, Sir!"

At midnight, fleeing my father
in the back seat of a Rambler
station wagon, life escapes
into my mother's bruises
as a sullen driver speeds us north.

Trumpet notes bloom
from the radio,
lodge into her clavicle,
breath upon breath.

At high speed, around
mountain curves
and miles of gravel
we hope to cross
the Sierra Madre before dawn.

Rancor for dreams left in the rains of Mexico City
settle into her eyes.

How will I survive this lower altitude
split in two,
our spirits vaporizing
into the rocks of the cordillera?

The cigarette smoke paths
she still craves in sleep
bind her fear — tattoo her face.

From this day forward,
her words,
full of hidden ordnance.

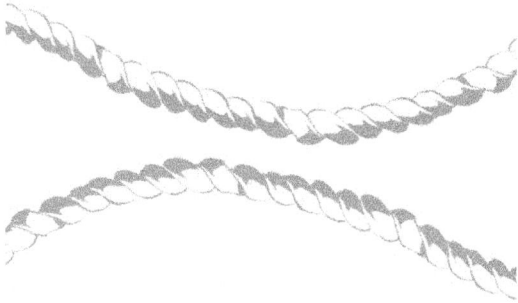

Shockwave

Fright
re-assembles your torso
from entrails to skin.

An earthquake feeds and sways
the mysterious giant
challenging your sky.

Scarce words,
out with the breath
solar plexus collapse.

Your jawbone sinks
to the root
of a Texas wild oak.

Your essence braces itself
against the bark, you bury
screams in the dirt and can't move.

An unseen raptor arrives,
spreads its talons,
scavenges the aftermath debris

and snatches you aloft
as if you were no more
than a tiny field mouse,

shakes its head with your feeble laments
bites off the appendages
of all you once knew to be true.

Sated, the owl
hoots and drops
you bloody

on new harbor planks.
Green and purple bruises
greet your new moorings.

Rope Luna Message 1

Mamá said:

Look out the car window.
You will not fall off the mountain.

Imagine a rope
from the moon

pulling you high,
lifting your body
away from the world.

Luna whispers through her rope:
nothing can touch you
expect me now and forever.

Tales of my Mother's Post-Partum

I didn't spoil her
dancer's body.

    A preemie, I left
    only a little sugar
    for her
    the previous star.

        A blessed time,
        at least that's what the family
        told her, the happiest
        of aches to be enslaved
        by diminutive
        new flesh.

I shone pink,
a new hoarder
of family love,

    all that attention
    for a tiny body that fit
    in the palm
    of my father's hand,

        a hand that later
        awakened her
        duty

        slapped her hard.

Texas Courtship in the Rio Grande Valley

I search for the thermos of pink
lemonade. The moccasin
swims the surface of the pond at my back.
Black satin poison and slither surprise
for the white man courting my mother
with a picnic on his ranch.

She tells me about the dignity of chaparral
and mesquite as the land yields
to a marsh with gray-brown and yellow birds,
anis, pygmy owls and kiskadees.
All this land for just a few cows
who still cross the border in the Rio
Grande Valley undisturbed.

He talks about the grasshopper infestation.

I tell myself she is an artist,
a ballet dancer
from Mexico City, she will never
bring me to live here.

His pearly buttons shine with the light
from the muddy water. He bends
casually for the morning paper,
only it's a rifle. He shoots the snake
in the head, its opalescent white mouth
flowers open for an instant
now a carcass of red and black
left for the vultures.

Welcome to Texas, he smiles,
home of the swimmer snakes.

Ven hija.

The Refuge of Trees

Texas Live Oaks twist trunks into long wayward branches
invisible closets to hold the terrors of a small girl
nestled between two large roots.
A safe brown embrace from the cruel playground
for an eight-year old
in jeans and maroon sweater.

No se habla español, no se habla español.
She rocks with her hands on either side of her face,
frames her cheeks in prayer, touches the folds of bark
and slowly curls into a ball.

The leaves form a vernal blanket
embed the wind
with a lullaby in green notes
and slowly drowns the sobs
in wheezes of crickets and cicadas.
Sleep, lilac flying dreams,
relaxes her shoulders.

Gnarled shadows chill the air.
White-tailed dove and cardinals return to the boughs
as the horizon begins to pocket the light
and darken this fallen child,
now an appendage of tree,
who doesn't hear her mother's frantic shouts,
and surely hums awake before morning.

Rope Luna Pull: Request 1

Elementary School Welcome:

My classmates said:
You stupid Mexican
go back where you came from!
I'll rip that sweater right off you.

Classmate's parents said:
This is a nice area why are you here?
They send the children of live-in maids
to the Mexican side of town.

The teacher said:
I don't have to give you "A's" in math,
I can give your kind any grades I want in third grade.

Mamá said:
Always listen to your teacher.

Quarry

As my torso grew, I kept the hero of *father* hidden
dreamt you could find me,
an undefended bloom
sprouting in a desert.

The years sharpened my internal planting
stick into an incisor
that still searches for depth;
stirs the mud around my feet
seeks the right sun and shade to belong.
The dream of you sleeps.

My quarry chiseled bone when I finally met you.

The gardeners that created me
moved away from their bodies.
My sepia shape, no longer confined
to the places my parents didn't stand.
I still can't find my door
in the labyrinth of white crosses.
I can't reach Mother's ghost in the mirror.

Red geraniums bloom for me, alone.

There is an ocean that comes and goes in its waves
discarding bone and wood,
the smooth glide of a canoe
on a glass river over tree shadows and trout,
there is a pilgrimage, a ritual of remembrance,
and I must find a metal file
to sharpen a new limb.

Skin needs Mother Armor

Too bad you can't inherit
my clothes; you are so fat.

My bruises don't come
from a shiny Texas buckle
or a slamming of the ribs
against a mahogany
table edge.

The purple Wandering Jew,
from my mother's garden
still not attached,

breaks in my hand.
Roots in water.

Mother creams her cheeks,
gazes in the mirror,
and decides on the expensive
couture she'll only wear twice.

Dark Mother

The living and the dead ask you Dark Mother of uncreated light,
what kind of *cuchillo* you use to cut a soul for rebirth?
The volcanoes of México provide the obsidian blade
that slices a new life into understanding.
Cucuy birds invade the air with instructions
on how to enter your pitcher of stars.

Black Madonna, I am here to assist.
I hear ice-voice skeletons shush shush in their gray world
and dance occasionally with an orange butterfly.
They reach out to you Mother, with a silver rope.

From our circle, we drum heartbeats
on goatskins to aid your summons.
Invisible beings ask for color.
I tell them they are ghosts
that require the return of your embrace
so the earth can learn their bones,
stories resting in dark rich clay.

Into a Texas Storm

Robin Blue for the front door,
strawberries on one side of the porch,
climbing coral tea roses
that survived enough winters
to interlace the trellis and reach the roof.
She closes the door behind her.
The silver key that locks
the dead bolt for the last time is still hers.

The marriage house is now a past
of scattered moonlight and curses
embedded in the curtains.

A place where carefully selected
window treatments

could not prevent dream sylphs
of a greener horizon from slipping
behind eyelids at night.

A Texas storm
is a torrent that claims instant ownership
naked in hope.
Drenched eyelashes form tiny triangles
and ears became miniature fonts.
The key slides into her pocket.
Gripping a small child in each hand,
she runs twenty footsteps to the car
pilgrims in a ferocious theater.

Tucson Desert Poppies

She's outlived all of her husbands.

She is just a bunch of chemicals now,
says my mother's friend.

> *She*
> *is not in her body.*

Her hair no longer
a dark exotic fan on the pillow,
cropped short to keep
tangles from her eyes.

I remembered Acapulco —

long-to-her-waist tendrils
      floating away from her body
           a mermaid frolicking the oceans
in search of a man to ensnare.

The desert poppies are in bloom at Picacho Peak.

The traffic lines up for miles
to see the short-lived
      red bleeds, guilt snakes
      lost
in the shadows of sahuaro.

My Father's Tree in a Land that Calls Me Home

The tree bark grooves inward,
elbows pointing in all directions —
A Coos Umqua tribal dance.
It remains a home for portent birds
who remember the lives
of our ancestors and tune
the wind in its dance.

The day of my father's heart failure,
three western screech owls arrive
to linger nightly in the downward slope
of the lower boughs,
until he dies.

My mother's stroke holds her frame rigid
from December to July,
her birth month.
In my father's tree three desert
pygmy owls come to wait for her.

My father's aether hand touches her brow
beckons through twig latches,
stark and visible in moon shadows
and pulls her spirit
from the wreck that is her body,
leaving a whiff of ancient forest
in the room where I sleep.

I expect the brown eyes of the barred owl to fly me home.

Planted in June 95 years ago,
the incense cedar, my father's birth tree,
scents the southern wind.
A branch once sliced by lightning,
is now a navel, layers deep
in the sap of its life.

SECTION 2

THE GOOD DAUGHTER

Rope Luna Message: 2

*Just because she only obsessed about her own story
does not give you a pass on being a good daughter.*

After the Stroke

Her nurses 'semi-caring'
hands move my mother's body
to avoid bedsores.

She speaks Spanish, French
and English with no translation.
Her monolingual therapists

do not understand.
Imperious in her tubes,
she cries, ¡*Basta*! Enough.

I tell her daughters grow
inside cacti, the world still
needs gypsies, children happy stories.

I trace veins, hold her age-spotted hand
but the bedrails can't contain
her body as it shreds.

She is the stubbornness of a heel
ground into the dirt.
The dark and light twine of her DNA

burn through
as when a drop of bleach
stains blue linen.

Night Duty

Mother!
calls out, confusing me
with my grandmother
dragging the 'r' sound
in a determined *come-to-me* plea,
exasperation in the long consonants.

She wanted milk.
A rouge liquid rises
from the needle in her arm,
a blemish on the nightgown and green sheets.

Mother!
calls attention to her discomfort while
hope drools from her mouth,
the *"change-me"* imperative hiss that says
appearances still matter.

My clothes forever stained
with cranberry and grape juice
as I feed her.
Pain pills pulverized
look like cocaine
mixed in the applesauce
she will not swallow.
Instead, she bites the spoon.

Mother! she says again,
The oxygen machine gasps
as she yanks away the tube.
She is hitting me.
Geriatric psychiatrist comes.

Over and over, she says *I hate you.*
Ten minutes later she begins to fall asleep
with her hand relaxing in my clasp.
My mind is on my childhood,
her mind is focused on breathing.
Mother —
you love me?

Speaking to the Moon Through the Kitchen Window

Jaguars with yellow eyes dream
me into the speed and agility
needed to race away and avoid a zoo.

I know deep within
we all live in cages
gilded by our own blood jailors.

This rattles my ribs.
I am more than competent at weaving
blue ribbons through cell doors
and pretending it's sky.

My asylum is a strong fortress
passionate and never frivolous —
with books lining the left wall.

Alas, I am still far from the jungle
too far from a Mayan *Cenote*
with depths that give me a way out.

Curandera Dream

I slice my finger
next to the tomato
blood mingles with

cilantro, cebolla, chile.

A revolution on my plate
blood and food —

My *curandera* interprets this dream
as the wrath of a Mexican
woman taught to suffer well.

Life's little lies
steal away from the body. Inner
brutalities that demand release.

cilantro, cebolla, chile.

Accidental slice
or purposeful bleed?

Rope Luna Message: 3

Doubt and bitterness are luxuries
your guardians should not have allowed.

Why have you waited years
to heed your spirit guides?

Your calling requires a Temascal
at least once a year.

Only a sweat lodge ceremony
can re-birth your inner child.

The Good Daughter

Care for my mother is ten thousand
pricks of yellow roses,
star-shaped scars
settled over time
in bruise blooms.

I position the flashlight
on her model looks —
the ballet star,
with her legendary ability to find beauty
in the plainest twig or sparrow.

Spoken fractures
like broken geranium stems
today drown
my best intentions
of living in the moment.
I stroke her forehead
with bitten fingernails.
I whisper ballet steps: *glissade, jeté, pas de bourrée.*

The cleansing of my catacombs
is like the sliced onions
I gently burn
white to clear
in hot olive oil,
for her favorite omelet.

The Transition Moment

Alone, constant lights,
people breathe in forgotten bodies
and unconsciously yearn
for a peaceful darkness
in a garden without pain.

The soul remains encased
by the wonders of medical engineering
inside flesh.
And yet there comes a moment,
a palpable pause,
when life's stings
make a final recording
within the skin-housed journey.

An immigrant's passage opens
to the side of an angel,
a promise of rest.

The self-taught bondage
of existing in a world in constant motion
and the daily torments
that occupy days

are left behind in the sheets.

The best of one's unique self
flies out of the body
steps inside a canoe
beside soft river water.

Tribal roots release to the flow
and heavy comfort
of death's slender hand
and an alder tree whispers,

awaken, you'll be fine.

Rope Luna Pull: Request 2

Guide me in this river.
My brother's hand no longer mine to hold.
Bone ash buried.

My daughter's breath,
is arrested in madness.

My son wars with himself
to find his way from my side.

The Ancestors freely reign
the dreamscape, weigh me with duty.

My skin still clings to its frame,
haunted.

Invocation

I am asleep when the door of the armoire closes itself,
hides half of the natural jade Oaxacan urn.
The blue shoe with its cracked heel
walks away from its pair in the closet,
ends up in the living room. Does it remember
its last trip to México where it almost fell
in the canals of Xochimilco?

Like the abruptness of moonrise in the desert,
the bathroom door closes unheard in the middle
of the night, locks from the inside.
No one is there.

I search my drawers
for the master key I keep hidden
for just such emergencies.
Unlocking the white pocket door,
I find my medicines pulled from the drawer
scattered on the floor. Abstract composition.

Who visits?
Is it the scent of my dead brother,
now one with his cigarette?
I last saw him feeding my daughter
spaghetti at Thanksgiving
and in a coffin before Christmas.

Is he searching for the lock of dark brown
I stole from his head
so stoically laid out at the funeral home
inside the white satin of a casket?

I placed his hair remembrance
beside the St. Jude
candle on my home altar,
along with a prayer to the saint
dedicated to recovering the hopelessly lost.

Is it Marina, my dear friend from Buenos Aires
who said the breasts they removed from her first
cancer were not the ones smoking now?

She had beautiful oval fingertips
that snuffed candles into smoke spirals —
so much like her life.

Barely visible white fingers click the computer keyboard in my study.

Through a muted night light,
I see one index fingertip on the question mark,
the other on the number sign,
pressing in rhythm, first one
and then the other,
over and over in a Morse code
for no ear,
no message on the screen.

The Seri Shaman Dreams the People

More dead Indians, a blackbird's caw.

Corn turns to stone
and we, the people of Atom Achai
have lost our connection to the great spirit.

        Our dream names have scattered.

The hummingbirds refuse to lighten
our spirits on the breeze at night.
The original people to come from the sea
struggle as prey in a raptor's beak.

 It has been five thousand years
              since we walked into the desert.

The deer still graze,
the coyotes still laugh, but we are
shadow-spiders under cottonwoods.

        The arrival of Spanish-and-English
           speaking condors

plucked the language from our tongues.
We watched while they scalloped
the earth into a leached cone.

Copper mines leaked

and turned the moon green.
The ants now refuse to carry our burdens
one corn silk at a time.

The toil of centuries dissolves

into green and red feathers,
grief mangled driftwood and sea foam.

White butterflies flee

the braids of our children.

The only remaining sanctuary
is under rocks tumbled by waves,

a drum song

beneath
the left breast of a Seri woman.

Visiting my Parents at Pioneer Cemetery
Yoncalla, Oregon

I am again in the cradle,
lost without you.

Why do we miss to whom we belong;
the misplaced longing of a blue iris?

The earth reclaims your vestiges
side by side in marble squares
staring at each other.

Father, you gave your genes
but discarded me.
I reminded you of my mother.
I am not the woman
who thwarted your fame,
rebounded time after time
from the slapping red of your huge hands,
remarried other men
who learned her curves,
and bought good bourbon
during trips to Costa Rica.

Mother, I am trapped in the refraction of your mirror,
the world circling your make-up table
where I lived like Snow White
in a tiny corner of silver painted glass,
armed only with a notebook and blue pen

I need the courage for a new
botanical garden where I choose
the order of petal and plant.

What is this bitter orange rind called grief?
This new philosophy of a single owl
feather no longer soaring?

Hasta Siempre/Until Forever

I let go of my son the way an ocean
gives up a whole sand dollar to the beach,
and then retreats to noise and froth
against the rocks.

Twenty years walking on parent glass
to learn the ocean cannot
be nailed to the shore.

Children cannot be contained
by goodness or right intention.
Their eyes see through a blinding fog
to a road where I cannot name the trees.

He is now on his own tarmac
flying through the doors
I placed around his body
when he could not walk alone.

The mother conch is empty,
sand fills the center-pink womb.
When he returns, I hope
he finds home again in the grey
of my hair and the lines of my face.

Rope Luna Message: 4

You thought your body wouldn't scar?

You can't be as thirsty
as a bleeding bull

in a ring
sword in his back

falling on his knees
before a matador.

Shells Unhinge

Death is unkind to the living,
so many poem caskets to decipher.
We should die the way a snowflake
softens on the horn of an elk,
and not be smashed under its hooves.

Cancer holds the smallest bones accountable
with its unique barbed wire.

Near the severing time
life becomes anecdotal —
a delicious green corn tamale,
a Neruda ode, a measured walk
in small steps to the Ocotillo in bloom.

Each of us owns a common memory
with the same poster in our offices.
Hopi *hermanas* holding hands,
dancing in turquoise long skirts,
in throes of joy.

The smoke of your baptism candle
is now tarnished silver
along your vertebrae.
It will not be dislodged by a chemo-therapy
so cruel it kills before the disease
grants final penance.

The bivalvia shell is now open,
its hinge intact between its two halves,
tossing its flesh to the waves
but still together, embracing.

Dream So Tired

What bends
underfoot is loneliness
every flattened blade of grass
individual, yet tied to the root tribe,
except for the weed— a night terror
from a hidden volcano
spoiling the view,
spill unchecked.

You smash
the pillow over your head
as nightmares leach the rest
from the back of your neck.
The past vanishes like background piano notes
heard but not memorized.

An unnamed tune
lingers and leaves to speak
with the spirits at the foot of your bed.
Does the cotton daze of dawn
spill into the curved fingers of morning writing
holding a purple pen, overrunning the white
page with family leftovers
forgotten in some electric spasm of nerves.

Awake, dream remnants
mix with your memories
and show up like a yearbook,
baby shoes, snippets of hair
and faces torn from photographs.

An album no one remembers,
a flash sequence of people no longer alive
dressed in pale silver who follow you around all day.

Night arrives
once more,
and the dark silence
entices relief and makes the nudity
of the days easier to clothe in sleep.
The newly dead gather around the bed and wait
to add their heaviness. The dreams begin
again to spew their lava.

You stand
before a precipice
of the past and the now,
and the mind requests action.
Do you cut the tulip, the iris,
the yellow rose?
Your body is inches away
from becoming the souvenir in a fire.

José's Roses

The first time José planted Mexicali Tea Rose cuttings, my grandmother Yaya, had to read the instructions while he worked. Never mind that he had to grow them under the toxic haze of *Avenida Tacubaya*, or take on the altitude of Mexico City. Pearl and blue hedges of tuber roses were planted in rows the way José plants his corn. It took hours to explain that they were ornamental, had to be staggered, to hide the view of the vegetable garden.

Every Saturday, José prays over the Shringar Rose, the fallen fragrance in the petals caressed like rosary beads between forefinger and thumb. Each clipped leaf and blossom lost to the wind is placed inside the *manta mochila-bag* he carries over the left shoulder. The contents gather at the end of the day on a compost pile.

Not until we see him bend over so far that his white hat touches the ground, do we hear his cry. Five years of savings stolen from under his mattress while his wife shopped for *bolillos* for the evening meal. It was to be an earthquake-proof large room, built of gray brick cement blocks, a bathroom attached.

SECTION 3

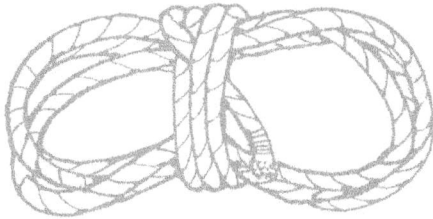

IF NOT, WINTER

If Not, Winter

after Sappho-Tanka in Hopi

If not winter, die
in a different season,
do not match the ice,
leave your body in summer
marry the harvest of blue corn.

> If not, winter cuts
> the stamen of cold mercy,
> calla lilly in
> a vase, death's intricacies
> enveloped in white bitter.

If not winter, red
boulders in Sedona seek
not to cup snow or
sing the wind for raven's flight,
shade for the *gold-sandaled dawn*.

> If not, winter in
> our ribcage awaits the moon
> *Múi'ingwa*, the time
> for germinating spirit,
> and flute to play new freedom.

If not, winter brings
flash lightning and yellow eyes,
cumulus clouds and
thunder where the weary fear
the untamed sound, death's eagle.

Brother Cardinal Sings to my Garden

Brother, I'm dreaming your nightmares again,
trapped in a circular script of war
in Bosnia, Mogadishu and Haiti,
countries that no longer
remember your footsteps.
Your terror is already cellared
in the earth,
payment is in your bones.

Sister prayers
no longer reach you, redbird.
The asters have fallen,
your breath's tattoo
turns us blue.
The blood chord
that connects us to your voice
has drowned,
now the measured silence
between slow drumbeats.

Our dream hands full of lavender
massage your temples,
salve the phantasms in your eyes.
We pray the angels
with white fiery swords
cauterize your memory.

Hermano,
remake your horror
into a new primeval Eden.
Ask for fresh flesh,
a black walnut cradle
within a family
that loves the smell of dark newly turned soil.

Adopted Daughter: Missing

She is Gone.
Now her absence,
is a night-wrench death
a non-stop mash inside the skull.

Her flight
black crow at my window.

> I touch the red-ribboned energy
> that binds our torsos —
> a bloodied finger, a gash.

> Her genes demand she
> search her biological imprint,
> the voice I call,

> the whore of cells.
> The devotion of years
> eroded by thieving blood.

This Mother cannot compete.

Rope Luna Pull Request: 3

What more of my flesh can be eaten?

Time is stolen from my breasts
I need rest.

I don't want to be conquered.

Arias for the Haunted

A false disguise for a daughter
whose brain chemicals ran amok
and ruined me,
       the mother in me,
          the human,
and replaced it with a holocaust
inside muscle memory.

                I am a flute
         a hollow reed with holes for notes
           not bothering the wind
            for sound or movement.

The body works,
      but the music of the desert stars
fades into a rattler's
      nest within *acequia* rocks.

            I try the hummingbird prayers —
         its ruby throat and rapid green darting
                  hook my breath.

Bait enough beauty to hear a small aria
      in the curl of a leaf.

Accidental Observer

Grandparents.
Gone.
Parents.
Gone.
Children
Gone.

The ancestors confused the stars
of her birth chart and gripped the curve of her clavicle
to keep her ribs upright while attending funerals.

She's the leftover stuck on a perch,
not solid enough to hold her weight or weave
her cactus skin into a new patchwork of days.

Now the mirror reveals a conch
cut in half its labyrinth exposed —
entry and exit the same route.

She is the accidental observer
tasked with chronicling their human stardust
and devastating lives.

A bone-blind Sephardic journey
of scarcity and shadow awaits
language that needs black ink

and reams of paper
before she too, can run barefoot
on the sweet green grass of summer.

The Seri and the Ironwood Tree

I.

The Zapotec Tule tree of Oaxaca
is a venerated 4,000 year-old guardian

that forever breathes
resistance to conquest and decimation.

The Seri Shaman scours the floor beneath ancient wings
to find one twig ambassador

to plant its remembrance song
in the sand of the Sonoran Desert shore.

Tourists leave perfectly trimmed
boxwood hedges to touch an ageless

hunger found within carvings
and fetishes made from holy ironwood limbs.

Thousands of totems shaped into quail,
hawks and deer

by idle Seri hands, who can no longer fish
among oil tankers and debris.

Immortalized spirit helpers sold at markets
until world demand ate all the trees.

The Seri and the Ironwood Tree

II.

The planted Tule twig moistens with ocean mist,
softens the light within the fog and summons

the memory of ironwood with sacred incantations.
The Shaman's entreaty

entices the gusts,
persuades hidden ironwood seeds

to return and uncurl forgiveness
for the last of the Seri,

who once rode with Turtle
in the beginning breath

and walked naked and pristine
as coral reefs hummed along the coast.

Dead Poets Return

In the silent pauses
before a new body's story begins,

the dream mementos that create a poet
emerge white and blind

out of a rare desert snow
side-stepping rusty scythes

and pottery shards.
A shade of blue

held by muses
in the boundaries of stars

waits until a chosen one's eyes open
in an innocent language womb.

The bones of new fingers
will be taught to strum calla lilies

on a cloud guitar
and macaws will harmonize a new fate.

Duende.

A New Pond

I want to be the gentle gnaw on apple skin
a brown mark on yellow flesh – still delicious.
More than just bread crumbs on pink lips
or a passing light on stones
that warms hardness.

A Kokopelli flute
to play silhouette against
an orange harvest moon.

I want purple and teal to be primary colors,
explain why I am a Degas
among Warhols. A *gitana*
who turns each day's iron nails
into appreciation for the discordant.

I can be a love nude
unblemished, without scissor scars,
with a word trail in my wake
that outlasts gray's mediocrity.

The sound in an un-tunable tuning fork,
the creator of green verbs
that vibrate beyond dreams.

I will be a lavender jacaranda blossom
who kisses the sun
and then falls asleep by yellow
patches of moon on Saltillo tile.

Rope Luna Message: 5

You can be conquered.

So what?

Your ancestors got up and walked,
so can you.

Un-Mothering

Scratches from a jumping-cholla cactus
further carve my face
into a mask; my hands
into calloused pads.

        I let go of the daughter-nails
           festering in my *Chi*.

The dawn witch
used a delicate gold
hammer's claw
to pull abscessed thorns
from my arteries
avoiding permanent holes
in the heart.

        Careful extraction
        replaced the pain vacuum
        with better night vision,
        a complex gift
        of new hawk eyes.

Manageable bleeds lessen in time
with beautiful jazz,
stranger kindness,
and crows taking flight before my steps.

        Recovery can take
        as long as the growth
        of a sahuaro,

        this life and the next.

Ode To Death

After Denise Levertov

I must be your lover for you visit often.

       Just when the flesh craves the freedom
         of weightless remembrance,
        the knee grinds into its cartilage;
      and headaches return to stand guard.

We don't even have the sense of geese
to fly counter to a storm.

         Instead, continue to believe
        the breeze conjured prayer
        of the redwoods of Muir

we are not just erased chalk
we are not just erased chalk —

The lacquered loneliness
of growing older
is like the frugality of kindness
in a large city.

         Encased in concrete
       the wind is a wolf's tongue
         caressing its teeth
      savoring the fog that walks
       inside the truant people.

Death should not be a craving,
it is the promise of the red maple leaf pretending
to be preserved in ice
after a storm, until it melts.

Shard

Daughter-Lover-Sister-Mother
is a broken shard next to an ancient ruin.
A geometric pattern
displaced from the whole.

At night, she tucks green pillows and magenta blankets
around her torso,
becomes a barnacle of soft fabric.

The legends of love no longer rise to fondle her skin.

She craves rest from duty stones.

She is a woman wrapped inside the
fringe *rapacejo* of a *rebozo*,
waiting for a shroud.

Once, she was a red and black clay story.

Now she dreams of unmasking the savagery
of male gods threaded in silk.

Rattle

Remember the priest who told you sex
as loving didn't count unless there were children,
even if they should starve or leave
you like a remnant towel turned to rags.

In this amber breathing, a rope of luna fiber descends,
curved at one end like a crescent.
Raven finally picks the wicker free
of the chair perch, focuses
his yellow eyes on your hands
and snatches the writing pen from your story.
He flies out the window and will not return.
The spring in the wood goes underground
to find its mother.

Face has been shut tight,
cobweb lines etched on a face that catches nothing.
Still have to find stones for the fire ring,
but need so much more heat just for one.

And then the cord your parents buried
in the earth at your birth
rattles in the ice of night.
Ants don't creep up through the cracks anymore.
No more sugar in the house, the right sugar.
The water cascade you crave
falls on your chest, holds you still.
Your time is near.
Get a coat.

SECTION 4

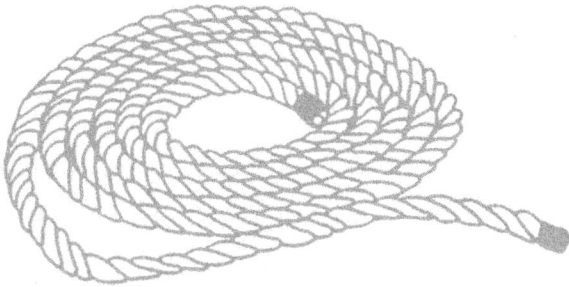

GATHER

One Day at a Time — Night Battles

Mourning has its own private hunger.
you can no longer be the salmon
who has laid its eggs in the shallows
and waits for the fisherman.

You must arise competent,
wear a black suit to keep appointments,
don the pink silk scarf
into a smile for your colleagues.

Pretend the office of paper clips
and computer clicks is actually friendly
and wish everyone you see a sincere good day.

Bats collect all day
to hang upside down in your ribcage,
to dissolve at nightfall.

Sleeping pills thicken the futility
into heavy shoulder pads
that pin you down
like a Luna moth in a gray box.

The mahogany yoke of sanity is unreachable.
In tornado dreams
your life force battles
to stay upright.

The next morning and the next morning and the next morning
for a very long time.

A Poet of Silver at 50

Now is a silver time
strung tight with deer hide,
empty of most duty contents

no longer a blade nicking the throat in its hurry.

A white apron of under-songs
surrounds every breath,
every step, every word.

Your pelvic fern radiates wisdom thunder-light.

Icicles melt in your mouth before their cut can pierce another voice.

No more remnant dull fabric
only bright colors
for the selenium wisps that frame your face.

The shadow caresses of a palo verde branch
whisper more clearly in your ear
on the remaining path
where no effort is wasted,
no gain reversed.

The second fifty moon years
wait for the stories you choose to share.
You are like the Jews who fled Toledo
during the inquisition
carrying the key from their homes in Spain
into the Americas.

On this birthday, the Maya natives bless the roads you have travelled.
Your prayers in the new world attune to the desert.
At once, a yellow monarch butterfly, lands on the mesquite
by your shoulder
a green throated hummingbird, flies to the nectar of a saguaro
and a cardinal, launches from a bird of paradise.

Rope Luna Pull Request 4

Remember breasts touched?

New moon.

Body scarred,

skin cellulite round.

Don't collect Luna Moths.

Blind Date, Angels in Tow

I.

Our guardian angels air kiss across the table,
then get right down to business
comparing our quirks and weaknesses.

They ceremoniously drape purple cloaks
made from past life scars over our shoulders
as we toast each other with that first glass of Shiraz.

The waiter brings a steaming dish of blue foolishness.
I suggest we breakfast with our devils.
Neither of us orders dessert.

II.

We make love in their presence
My date bends to nibble
the resistance in my left nipple.
For years, I've collected bruised marble
under that latch.

My angel has nagged me
to buy a broom and sweep out
the dead moths and cut stained glass,
shove it into the pink dust pan
and toss it once and for all.

I have not done so.

His guardian angel whispers
in a voice reminiscent of Rumi,

all meaning translates into
a ton of bricks falling on your head.

Try to heal by reading in bed.

You are hopeless!

Skin Hunger — *Hambre de Piel*

I now hold so much of your breath
inside my pores
it has begun its own life.

    My fingers massage your brows
    and the small round movements around your temples
    are questions I know you can't or won't answer.

        But I wish I could speak up
        and grant you the sexual favors you seek
        without being wooed.

I would rather you not know
how the coral reef of regrets
connected to my spine feels nude,
is hesitant to be overtaken
by a cloud that vapors my tongue
like chile habanero.

    Later I will sit under a magnolia tree
    in my garden among red pyracantha
    berries in full bloom
    noting how beauty and poison
    willingly share space.

        Hambre de piel
        the skin hunger of steep vulnerability.
        You, who moisten my fingertips
        with your smile
        until invisible ostrich feathers ignite a fear
        that until recently,
        was under house arrest.

Your kiss,
like the last taste of soup
chasing the spoon round and round in a bowl.

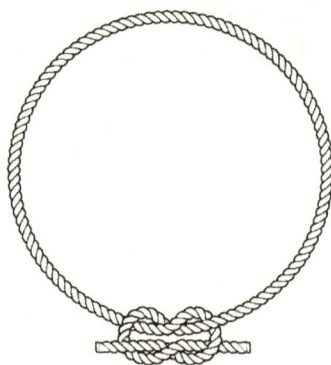

Dating Journal

"If I can't find love, If I can't find peace, give me a little glory,"
— Anna Akmatova

One Evening:

How long before desire is not buried in sleep?
Before the mandated conversation about our history
trots the skeletons from our closets
sits them down on the antique love seat
to tell the stories of their leached bones?

How long before the tip of the vocal whip
is snapped in anger, creating a new gash
on a stitched heart,

before the unsaid becomes rocks
carried in our childhood backpack,

before love is strung on a line of caught fish?

Another Evening:

How long before our mundane faults emerge,
about how to shine wash dishes,
arrange the teal sofa cushions
or clean our indistinguishable hair from the tub?

I am the birch waiting for the forest
fire to reach my branches;

you are the loneliness in the wind
chasing the flames
until we both become something else.

One Morning:

How long before Evgen Bavcar captures
the shadow of imprisoned love in a photograph?

A part of me knows I could love you green,
but before I speak, what if this is only confusion
and never happens —

does not ignite the comet

we won't see for another hundred years?

How long before there are mismatched
black suitcases side by side at the door?

Rope Luna Message: 6

Unconscious attempts to grab my rope
when navigating normal gravity is unseemly.

Reconstitute the rags of survival.

Laugh.

Spirit splatter is still moon-dust
pollen inside the calla lily

falling on white petals
moved by a breeze.

One Red Brick

All the white walls in the world
have one red brick that warps monotony.

It is the moment patience unhinges its belly coil.
It is a heaven or hell in stucco stance.

Someone you don't know
defiles it like a Nazi.

No one, you also don't know,
does anything.

A matter of free speech
that officials repaint white.

If the pear that is your body
is corkscrewed into a green wine bottle,

the best label, years of grapes near the ocean;
the rest of the world would be tempted

to smash it against the white brick
because, how dare you?

The brick's gestures
are your collage of bruises,

a poetic signature with mortar lines
that disappears one cloudy day

away from walls, away from white
into carnations, wild and red.

Artists for Dinner

Artists
are the razor
that tempt the wrist.

The tiny mirrors
beneath their flesh
encompass unique luminosities —
distinct wicks of unshackled color
that play with light,
air, sound or canvas.

They dance to the arc of a Bonsai tree
and stare all day at crows on a fence
to capture the vacancy
in a human eye.

At dinner, artists are conversation
nomads wrapped in warm
loaves of bread.
They are cattails in a potato soup
who laugh and write opera
from the stones
they carry on their backs
bathed in vinegar and brine.

Meditation Walk in Santa Barbara

I decide to walk the Via Dolorosa
made by the Jesuits who once lived here,
a path no longer pruned and left to the wind.
The Stations of the Cross
were once paced every few yards
among the natural outcroppings
of the native trees.

When the property sold, the icons
were removed from their branch frames
and the trees shriveled and darkened,
misplaced in their purpose
without constant reverence and prayer.

I find a contemplation spot
between two trunks close together,
forming a "v". I sit inside the oak
cradle of a rough mother,
an open birth canal.

Standing upright between my feet
is a black feather
a fierce piercing of the packed ground
inches deep in the earth.

What inexplicable torque force
prevented a gentle swaying
in the wind to lie flat
on its side, when it reached
its rest on the earth?

The water in the arroyo surrounding my perch
has gone underground.
The rocks once rounded by the flow of water
have bleached white in the constant sun.
No more movement of rain or refraction of light.

The pebbles are now stagnant in their composition
within the cracked banks.
Among the sepia tones of dried
prairie grasses and brambles
I find my welcome —
a wild purple orchid dressed tall in green stalks.

Gather

Gather my hands now that they are spotted,
move slowly over the knots growing on the knuckles.
Grasp my fingers together as if they were scented tulips
emerging red from winter's hibernation.

Give me a shrine to record the stories
of a small boy abandoned to my care at birth,
today a grown man.
Remember my fingers bent in a loose curve
stroking your forehead to sleep,
or to close the eyes of your beloved grandmother
from this world to spirit.

Take my hands to the bark of a birch
to hear once again the lullaby of ants
and green wood bending to a gust.
Give me a virgin page and a purple pen
so that I may rediscover the white ledge of possibility.

Hold my scars so you don't repeat them.
Gather apple blossoms and place them
on my chest, beneath prayerful hands.
I won't forget, but one day,
you might long for their weight.

Still

A haloed moon behind window glass enters the bedroom
paints the pecan tree branches
venetian blind — sliced
on the wall by the bed.

In this wakeful moment,
history has no battles
over the white and grey territory of the room
no victories or losses over correct God.

Only a woman alone in a bed
clutching a forest green blanket
with itch-burn in her hands.
A woman who craves
a land not touched by graves,
a sanctuary for those who birth and care.

A haven of even breaths idled on a front porch
rocking away the seasons in steady rhythms —
blue jays stealing twigs
from the sky's silhouette,
no browning of winter
trees widening their canopies each year
near a river that swells with rain,
embraces the land
and never breaches its banks.

A place every mother becomes a Luna Moth
disinterred   iridescent   flying.

ACKNOWLEDGMENTS

Publication Acknowledgment:

"Texas Courtship" was first published by *Palabra Literary Magazine*, a Magazine of Chicano and Latino Literary Art. Edition 6, Palabra Publications LLC..

"Arias for the Haunted" was first published by *Mom Egg Review* Contributor 12.

"Ironwood," "Hasta Siempre" and "Artists for Dinner" were published by *Somos en Escrito*.

"The Day we Split in Two," *San Pedro River Review 2016*

"José's Roses," *Border Senses Review 2014*

"By the Time a Writer Turns 50," *Voices de la Luna 2016*

"Gather" Published by *Conch.es Review* in July 2017 issue.

ABOUT THE AUTHOR

Lisha Adela García is a child of the immigrant streams that form the Americas. She is a border mongrel with Spanglish, Mexico and the United States in her psyche and in her work. She has an MFA in Creative Writing from the Vermont College of Fine Arts and currently resides in Texas with her beloved four-legged children. Lisha also has a Master's degree for the left side of her brain from the Thunderbird School of Global Management. Her first book, *Blood Rivers*, was published in 2009 with Blue Light Press of San Francisco. Her chapbook, *This Stone will Speak*, was published by Pudding House Press in 2008. She has numerous publications in journals including *Crab Orchard Review, Mom Egg Review, Boston Review, Border Senses* and many others. Lisha is also a literary translator, editor and teacher. For more information, please visit her website at www.lishagarcia.com.

NOTES FOR: A ROPE OF LUNA

Texas Courtship In the Rio Grande Valley:
Ven Hija means: Come Daughter.

Dark Mother:
This poem is dedicated To Fr. Jorge Rodriguez Eagar, my teacher in so many traditions.

My Father's Tree in a Land that Calls me Home:
Dedicated to Shannon Applegate and Daniel Robertson.

Speaking to the Moon Through My Kitchen Window:
Cenote is a deep hole without bottom that was a fresh water source for Mayan indigenous people and was found in the jungle of the Yucatan Peninsula. In a blessing for the People, young women were sacrificed here to preserve the fertility of the earth.

Invocation:
Xochimilco is the location of the Aztec floating gardens, south of Mexico City and still in use today.

The Seri Shaman Dreams the People:
The Seris are an indigenous group from the Mexican state of Sonora that borders with Arizona. The Zapotecs are an indigenous people of Mexico concentrated in the southern state of Oaxaca.

Shells Unhinge:
Dedicated to my sister-hermana friends, Marina Sukup and Joyce Ulhir who both died of cancer within weeks of each other. Altar de Muertos is an altar created for the Day of the Dead commemorating departed family members, friends and loved ones.

José's Roses:
Avenida Tacubaya is a major thoroughfare in Mexico City. Mochila is a type of rucksack and manta is the most traditional hand-woven cotton fabric in Mexico. Bollilos are the most common form of daily bread; tear-shaped with a crunchy outside and a soft interior.

Hasta Siempre and Gather:
Dedicated to my son, Carlos Mariano.

If not, Winter, Tanka in Hopi:
Múi'ingwa is the Hopi deity of germination. The Hopi are a tribe in Northern Arizona. *If not, winter and gold sandaled dawn* are fragments of a poem by Sappho. Dedicated to Mary Fillmore.

Shard:
Rapacejo is the patterned fringe on a *rebozo*, a Mexican shawl. It is usually a snake pattern representing Quetzalcoatl, the plumed serpent.

Brother Cardinal Sings to my Garden:
Dedicated to my late brother, Rex Allen Applegate.

A Poet of Silver at 50:
On the path where no effort is wasted, no gain reversed is a quote from the Bhagavad Gita.

Dating Journal:
Evgen Bavcar is a renowned — and blind — Slovenian photographer.

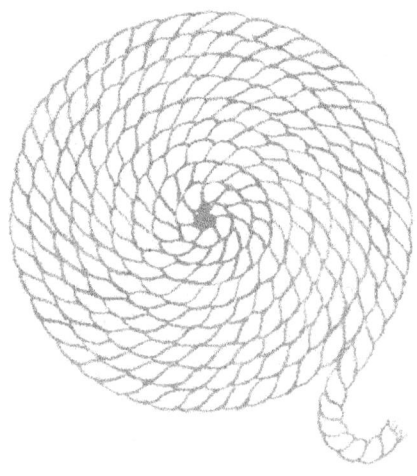

www.ingramcontent.com/pod-product-compliance
Lightning Source LLC
Chambersburg PA
CBHW032021090426

42741CB00006B/691